The Collection 2012

An Hachette UK Company
www.hachette.co.uk

First published in Great Britain in 2011 by Hamlyn,
a division of Octopus Publishing Group Ltd, Endeavour House, 189 Shaftesbury Avenue, London,
WC2H 8JY

www.octopusbooks.co.uk

Giles R is a registered trademark of Express Newspapers
Text and images copyright Express Newspapers 2010
Design layout copyright © Octopus Publishing Group Ltd 2011

ISBN 13: 978-0-600-62228-4

A CIP catalogue record for this book is available
from the British Library.

Printed and bound in China

10 9 8 7 6 5 4 3 2 1

The Collection 2012

EXPRESS NEWSPAPERS

hamlyn

Contents

An Introduction by

Adam Hart-Davis

The Giles Annual was a regular part of my childhood. From more than 50 years ago I can remember several favourite drawings. In the Christmas cartoon just after the M1 had been opened, Santa was driving his snorting reindeer at breakneck speed down the new motorway, with presents, snow, and motorists scattering behind. Following shocking news that trains might run on time, there was a glorious drawing of a country station, bowler-hatted commuters panting desperately up the hill, and a sign on the platform:

6.15 on time
7.05 ten minutes early
Next train GONE!

But the real joy with Giles lies in the detail of the drawings, and particularly with the cast of characters: pin-striped city gents, ministry officials, and bank managers; dusty teachers; solid flat-capped farmers; and the Giles family with snoozing dad, frumpy middle-aged women, girls with impossibly short skirts, kids, both innocent and evil, and always lurking somewhere Grandma, often asleep and about to be wired to the mains, or blasted off the face of the earth.

In this vintage collection there are as many strikes as in a box of matches: a bespectacled child carrying a fishing rod is politely saying in the staff room "If you please, Sir, this delegation offers the teachers' strike the whole-hearted support of the entire school" and then "The electricians' strike doesn't really affect us – Father does all his own electrical repairs" – while there is steam coming from the radio, the BBC Light Programme coming from the kettle, and Father has just connected himself to the mains…

May these annuals never stop.

Stinker

"If somebody don't quit overtime on that top 'Noel', somebody's going to find himself redundant."

Sunday Express, November 13, 1949

"And now, if the last boy to leave school on Nov 5 will kindly step forward..."

Daily Express, November 6, 1951

"Boys, boys – not all of us think of May the first as Labour Day."

Daily Express, May 1, 1952

"Whoever is popularising polo can't know what we already have to put up with from football and cricket."

Daily Express, June 11, 1952

"I read some interesting facts about education costing more than the police stations, fire stations, libraries, parks and highways all lumped together."

Daily Express, September 1, 1952

HOLIDAY CARTOON - A quiet picnic.

Sunday Express, August 30, 1953

"And now I want to present a little boy who's come along to represent the symbol of 1954..."

Daily Express, December 31, 1953

"Go and tell Dad we've discovered a Roman underground railway."

Daily Express, September 28, 1954

My whole-hearted sympathy to the Master of Foxhounds who complained of a "Pirate" pack poaching on his hunting grounds.
If you let one "Pirate" pack get away with it you'll get another, and another...

Sunday Express, January 16, 1955

National Safety Campaign No. 1

Daily Express, May 31, 1956

"Never mind what the archbishop will say – here comes Chalky."

Daily Express, January 16, 1958

"Sidney – did you put a bee in Miss Emily's Easter bonnet?"

Sunday Express, April 17, 1960

"Well I don't think this is better than spending the week-end in Aunt Rosie's stuffy front room."

Sunday Express, June 2, 1963

"Any Prime Minister who looks that much like Chalkie's has my vote."

Daily Express, October 24, 1963

"Frankly we DON'T think you were justified in calling out the combined R.A.F. – Police emergency squad because you thought he was going to belt you one!"

Daily Express, August 4, 1964

"If Willie can't drink a pint of old ale without getting pickled Willie won't be ready for the hard stuff next term."

Sunday Express, January 16, 1966

"And when I tell you they were probably running off to find a little church don't call me a silly old moo."

Daily Express, October 18, 1966

"Perhaps it was a little irreverent," said the Bishop about the verger who dropped a stink bomb in a joke shop ... "Especially as methinks the man from the joke shop has just lobbed one back."

Daily Express, November 9, 1967

"I expect the Queen's Park Rangers fans will be very cross when they find someone's hi-jacked their engine."

Sunday Express, January 5, 1969

"Vibrations from the 'Make War Not Love dept'. Grandma says if everybody isn't out of her bed in 3 minutes flat she'll be coming up to join you."

Daily Express, March 27, 1969

"Another marked difference between the Royal Family film and ours is they manage to get the top of their heads in for a start."

Sunday Express, June 22, 1969

"Quiet, boys – it's the Army taken over from the cops."

Daily Express, August 21, 1969

"They'd have their work cut out to corrupt some of mine."

Daily Express, July 7, 1970

"You have the honour of being elected by the committee to personally present our demands to Chalkie."

Daily Express, May 16, 1972

"We'd all settle down much quicker if they played a little less Mysterious East and a little more Hop Scotch."

Daily Express, September 5, 1972

"More industrial unrest – show him anywhere in the New Testament where it says Kings shouldn't tidy up after the donkey as well as Poor Shepherds."

Daily Express, December 17, 1974

"Just when did this vision that you were the New Messiah come upon you?"

Sunday Express, January 23, 1977

"Dad, Mum says would you like a mince pie while we're waiting for the fire brigade?"

Daily Express, December 24, 1979

"Patricia! No Lester Piggot tactics, please!"

Sunday Express, May 31, 1981

"Somebody kindly inform the lady that we are not muggers."

Sunday Express, December 12, 1982

"We hear you've been trying to flog your story for blood money of 'How I booked Chief Constable Gregory for parking one Sunday in '77.'"

Daily Express, June 28, 1983

"Hoots everybody! Grandma and her sister are back from their Over Sixties Hogmanay party."

Daily Express, December 31, 1984

"I'll do my best not to win, but if I lose I'll knock the stuffing out of you."

Sunday Express, July 13, 1986

"Beautiful, tranquil summer trip up the river – non-stop commentary of their first game of the season, blow by blow."

Daily Express, August 20, 1989

"We're changing the route – they'll find out when they get to Land's End."

Daily Express, April 21, 1991

Strikes

"Household Cavalry here, corporal, reporting for unloading duties."

Sunday Express, July 24, 1949

"If you please, Sir, this delegation wishes to offer the teachers' strike the whole-hearted support of the entire school."

Daily Express, April 4, 1951

"My dad reckons that anyone who has to spend all day with us ought to get the same as a Hollywood film star."

Daily Express, April 18, 1952

"Not in the widest sense, Wilkins, will I accept that Cinderella's Fairy Godmother was in any way an engineer."

Sunday Express, December 6, 1953

"The electricians' strike doesn't really affect us – Father does all his own electrical repairs."

Daily Express, January 19, 1954

"A Reverend Shop Steward to see you, Your Grace."

Sunday Express, March 17, 1957

"Never mind about it being time you knocked off for your token strike – pass me that ********** spanner."

Daily Express, March 21, 1957

"I'd rather get a rocket from the N.U.R. for not striking when they say 'Strike' than one from her Ladyship for striking when she says 'Don't.'"

Daily Express, May 9, 1958

"Did I hear you call me a blackleg, young fella?"

Daily Express, October 29, 1959

"Him Paleface picket – Him Redskin picket. They say we no shoot."

Daily Express, March 8, 1960

"Should be a good game."

Daily Express, January 17, 1961

"Tell Acker Bilk he's got his first fan mail – from the people next door asking when he's joining the Musicians' strike."

Daily Express, May 24, 1962

"It's worth a try."

Daily Express, July 23, 1964

"For the record – during yesterday's booking clerks' strike 5,982 passengers used this station. Net takings in the honesty box – one and ninepence."

Daily Express, March 16, 1965

"As I was saying, Bertha – not all of 'em wanted to return to work."

Daily Express, July 1, 1966

"Postal Workers' Union? They've got our chief counter clerk. If we strike I don't fancy his chances."

Daily Express, May 7, 1968

"As a BOAC pilot working his passage home – rival airline, tourist class – I can assure you the strike has not got 100 per cent support."

Daily Express, April 1, 1969

"Closing our local while we're on strike is not the kind of support we're looking for, laddie."

Sunday Express, July 26, 1970

"The newspaper strike is over – the papers are back and we're not playing 'I Spy' this morning."

Daily Express, September 24, 1971

"Sorry about loading your own gear, chaps – got a spot of industrial dispute with me crew."

Sunday Express, July 30, 1972

"Listen, mate, a whack from my missus is one thing – but one from yours is another."

Daily Express, April 25, 1974

"The hospital says that as you're a doctor working to rule you should know better than to break your ankle during the emergency."

Daily Express, December 8, 1975

"If you won't serve firemen when we're on strike don't you catch
fire when we ain't."

Daily Express, November 9, 1977

"It wasn't my fault you didn't go on TV because of the strike – stop sulking and eat your pud."

Sunday Express, December 24, 1978

"Which show did you say Bridget's new boy friend would have been on but for the TV strike – Eurovision or the Muppets?"

Sunday Express, March 11, 1979

"You, you and you – in here. You, you and you – hold on! They didn't tell us they were sending any from Holloway."

Daily Express, October 19, 1980

"That was very rude to tell Aunty that a couple of weeks at the coalface would make her think differently about the miners' strike."

Sunday Express, March 6, 1983

"I can't bear people who address me as 'Luv' – especially when they follow it up with a crack across the head!"

Daily Express, April 10, 1984

"It's not official yet – just a practice run."

Daily Express, April 17, 1984

"Thank the TV strike – missing your mooring and slipping into the Solent didn't make News At Ten."

Daily Express, August 8, 1985

"For the bad news – you've just winged Prince Philip. For the good news – the TV news people are on strike."

Sunday Express, January 4, 1987

"Just turn your back for a few hours' strike and they're off."

Sunday Express, January 10, 1988

"My dream honeymoon – sitting freezing for three days while you
play midfield for a knock-up team to pass the time."

Sunday Express, April 3, 1988

Rural Life

"The sun never sets on the British Empire, do it?"

Daily Express, April 29, 1947

"When you've finished discussing all this lovely machinery we're going to have in a few years' time, could you fetch me another piece of string?"

Sunday Express, August 24, 1947

"Seems like this one does not wish to sell his cattle to the Black Market."

Sunday Express, November 2, 1947

"That makes real good sense, don't it? I employ women to help out, then the men want to take time off to get married."

Daily Express, August 27, 1948

"Georgie – run and tell master the gentleman has called for the tithes."

Daily Express, April 20, 1950

"A few night-guard duties in Squire's woods'll help the meat ration – 'Halt. Who goes there?' No answer. Bang! And down comes a pheasant."

Sunday Express, November 18, 1951

"But if we didn't call up your men for the Forces, how on earth could we afford to lend you soldiers to help with your harvest?"

Daily Express, July 23, 1952

"People who take their children for holidays in Spain want to leave them there."

Daily Express, June 30, 1953

NOTE FROM FARMER GILES. Reading that the days of the "wicked-old-varmer-chasing-townsfolk-off-his-land" are over, and that a Farmers' Union spokesman announced that Britain's farmers WANT city people to visit their lands – as they would a factory – prompts us to illustrate an ancient legend concerning city visitors to the country. Asked by a visiting city gentleman why that cow had no horns, a farmer replied that there were all sorts of cows, some with long horns, some with short horns, some had crumpled horns, and some had no horns at all, but the real reason THIS particular cow had no horns was that 'twas a horse. There are, of course, lots of jokes about farmers visiting towns.

Daily Express, February 24, 1954

"'One man's meat...' as the saying goes, gentlemen."

Daily Express, May 4, 1954

"Never mind about your M.P. who said that children should be allowed to help on the farm and HIS little boy drives a tractor –
Git Off!"

Daily Express, February 9, 1956

DEAR PRINCE PHILIP – With reference to the bit in your speech where you said you were not sure whether farming was a profession or a pastime…

Daily Express, November 12, 1957

"Know what today is, young feller? September the twenty-ninth – known in the best farming circles as 'Muck Spreading' Day."

Daily Express, September 29, 1959

"They've published a letter he wrote telling 'em you know less about farming than his Aunt Fanny."

Daily Express, March 17, 1960

"Oi! Just a minute, Maverick."

Daily Express, December 5, 1961

"His good lady here doesn't think they can afford one this year"

Daily Express, December 8, 1964

"It may have been a rotten harvest, but I've improved my breast stroke."

Sunday Express, October 3, 1965

"I suppose now's as good a time as any – someone's just borrowed about five hundred of his turkeys."

Daily Express, December 15, 1966

"I think Harry's a little bit hurt – he didn't like the bit about Harry leading with the combine as there isn't anything slower than Harry."

Daily Express, December 18, 1969

"Your 15 per cent pay rise don't make you Chief Constable, Bert Jenkins."

Daily Express, November 2, 1972

"At the risk of running into trouble with the Sex Discrimination Act, your presence is required in yonder meadow."

Daily Express, December 30, 1975

"You'll have to do something about your weight, Thomas, potatoes are very fattening."

Daily Express, January 22, 1976

"Would you mind telling your wife to air her grievances on price increases to Mr. Peart and the Common Market and not to me."

Daily Express, March 8, 1976

"If any housewife comes complaining that a better deal for farmers means dearer food in the shops – I'm out!"

Daily Express, January 23, 1978

"I don't reckon the Governor would be very happy if he heard you'd got 5–1 with William Hill against us starting the harvest before Christmas."

Daily Express, August 15, 1978

"I just heard your boss say he's going to trade you in for a computerised, air-conditioned, articulated tractor."

Daily Express, December 4, 1979

"Try me on the option of a 'oliday in Balmoral or bringing in the 'arvest 'ome."

Daily Express, August 19, 1982

"Petrol up another 5p – don't go down to the pub in the Rolls, dear, or they'll all be hollering for a rise."

Sunday Express, September 12, 1982

"That was unfortunate, Willie – they're all in the feeding stuff business."

Daily Express, June 2, 1983

"On the other hand, if you don't let me through with my sheep you aren't going to get very far either."

Daily Express, February 12, 1985

"If there's one thing makes me anti-Establishment it's a farmer nudging me in the back when I want to go to sleep."

Sunday Express, June 1, 1986

"And my Party's manifesto will remove the BBC's ban on playing George Michael's sex record till after 9 o'clock."

Sunday Express, May 24, 1987

"I'm not having an extra litter a year to please him. Or you."

Sunday Express, May 20, 1990

Vicars

"This year, gentlemen, all catapults, air guns, squeakers, buzzers and so forth will be deposited with me and returned to you AFTER the carol singing."

Daily Express, December 15, 1946

"Very well! Heads we have the village hut for 'Comforts for Korea', tails you have it for the anti-atom brigade."

Daily Express, August 1, 1950

"Father says providing he ain't called up, sold up or blown up, he'll be delighted to be Santa Claus at the kiddies' party."

Daily Express, November 16, 1951

"Vicar! On behalf of the Cornflower Water Colour Group I protest that allowing the Friends of Asia Painting Society to use the village hall the same day as us is carrying peace too far."

Sunday Express, April 12, 1953

"Somebody has got to get through and explain to his lordship that we have not come to steal his turkey."

Sunday Express, December 13, 1953

"That's settled then, Vicar – all you have to do now is slip round and tell the Lady Dowager that little Miss Whatsit's going to open the fête instead of her."

Daily Express, July 6, 1955

"Before I was reformed, if anyone had told me I'd be on this game for Christmas I'd have nicked his ******* ear orf."

Sunday Express, December 4, 1955

"A few burst pipes and a power cut pack 'em in better'n all the sermons, eh, Vicar?"

Sunday Express, February 5, 1956

"Ask vicar if we can have first and last verses only so you can get home for the England v U.S.S.R. match?
I most certainly will NOT!"

Sunday Express, June 8, 1958

"'Ullo, Vicar, we didn't know you was in Lunnun for the Smithfield."

Daily Express, December 11, 1958

"If the Summit talks fall through, calling him Dwight Nikita Harold is going to make him look pretty stupid."

Sunday Express, August 30, 1959

"May we assume that we owe this honoured and most welcome visit to the possibility of your favourite TV Western going on strike?"

Sunday Express, February 12, 1961

"I certainly will not offer a special prayer that your inside right plays a better game next week than he did yesterday."

Sunday Express, August 19, 1962

"Even so, that's no way to talk to Vicar when he asked if he could expect your usual contribution to harvest festival."

Sunday Express, September 5, 1965

"Like I said – give 'em an inch they'll take a yard. Yesterday it was 'Can I try your crash lid on?'"

Daily Express, November 23, 1965

"Some say he got his ear bitten by a scrum half in the match against St. Mark's, others say he made an unchurchmanlike pass at Miss Flute the organist."

Daily Express, October 30, 1966

"Another big spending spree before the Budget – about three ha'pence a head."

Sunday Express, January 21, 1968

"You make the same mistake in the judging as they did with Miss England, boy, and I'll maim you."

Sunday Express, May 18, 1969

"Nude models may be all right for Carnaby Street, Mrs. Barker, but not for the Ladies O.S. Stall, St. Botolph's Jumble Sale."

Sunday Express, June 1, 1969

"It is most certainly not time for Service yet, madam – I suggest a junior member of your family has put your clock a few hours forward instead of one hour back."

Sunday Express, October 31, 1971

"Actually Charlie has read the notice, but that lamp he picked up was a trifle warm."

Daily Express, February 8, 1973

"A word before you go, Mr. Thomas – about the coach trip I hear you're organising to see this Last Tango."

Sunday Express, February 18, 1973

"Well that's all right lads. 11.0 Matins; early lunch; kick-off 3.0; back here by 5.30; wash and brush up and a cup of tea; Evensong 6.30."

Daily Express, January 8, 1974

"Go ye forth and speed the gospel to our flocks and at all times keep your eye on the Fuzz"

Sunday Express, May 11, 1975

"I must say a Reverend 36-24-36 wouldn't be a bad idea, eh Harry?"

Sunday Express, July 6, 1975

"You'd better get it across to that flock of yours that a little inflation in the kitty won't do any harm."

Sunday Express, February 20, 1977

"Morning Charlie. I hear thou didst commit a sin that passeth all understanding by thrice placing the ball in your own goal during the first match of the season."

Sunday Express, August 20, 1978

"Right! Who locked Vicar in the cupboard after service on Christmas Day?"

Sunday Express, December 31, 1978

"Daddy, I think Mrs. Montpelier-Smythe heard you say, thanks to her rock cakes, building may now commence."

Sunday Express, July 15, 1979

"I wish Vicar hadn't read our new Archbishop breeds the wretched things."

Sunday Express, September 9, 1979

"Reminding daddy that the Pope can pack Wembley with a crowd as big as the Cup Final does nothing for Christian Unity, Prunella."

Sunday Express, May 30, 1982

"I think calling the farmers a conniving bunch of hedge and tree slashers in your first sermon was perhaps unfortunate."

Sunday Express, September 30, 1984

"I think they heard you say they'd make a better Bonnie & Clyde, Vicar."

Sunday Express, December 22, 1985

Olympic Games

"Grandma! For heaven's sake forget there's a grandma competing
in the Olympic Games – you're too late for the selectors, anyway."

Daily Express, August 18, 1960

"Well – there's two Antonios who have no doubts about
whether the British Team girls are girls or not."

Sunday Express, August 23, 1960

"For you, Archie – the Editor wants you to cover the protest march on Sunday."

"Bad enough them holding their Olympics same time as us."

Sunday Express, September 10, 1972

"Do you think we could take one with a little more Olympic fire to show the Joneses when we get home?"

Daily Express, February 9, 1976

"On your mark! This is the best chance we've had of winning a Gold yet."

Daily Express, July 20, 1976

"Thank goodness he didn't win – we'd never have got him up on the top one."

Sunday Express, July 25, 1976

"Like Kennedy Airport banning the Russians – if you don't let 'em in, they can't beat you."

Daily Express, February 12, 1980

"Comrade Ivan want to know if it's true the Iron lady's ordered the British Leyland brass band touring Japan to commit hara-kiri if they don't win?"

Sunday Express, July 20, 1980

"If they all withdrew I'd look on it as a step towards world peace."

"Latest report on the school hols front – they've all gone out to buy Olympic javelins."

"She wrote to the shoe people and said she'd watch the Olympics in her bare feet for half the price, but they turned her down."

Daily Express, July 31, 1984

"If he once mentions the Olympic Games or tells us we're all runners in the great race against evil, I'm withdrawing to the Spotted Cow."

Sunday Express, August 5, 1984

"Awake, Perseus – if you can go as fast as Tessa Sanderson's javelin, you might just catch the 7.10."

Daily Express, August 9, 1984

"Very well, I'll just let you hit Michael Whitaker – then I don't want to hear any more Olympics for the next four years."

Daily Express, August 14, 1984

"Nothing to do with the Olympic Games – they're in training to get back to work in the Daily Express next week."

Daily Express, September 22, 1988

More great titles from Hamlyn

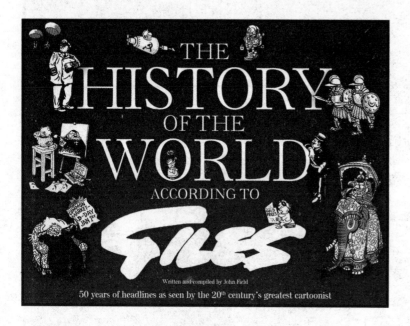

For over 50 years Giles documented and satirised the most momentous events in British and world history. Now, in one special collection, you can relive some of the greatest news stories through the artistry and wit of your favourite cartoonist. See the world through the genius mind of Giles, and go back to school with a wonderful romp through British life, from politics to family, education, the world of work and more.

The History of the World According to Giles
978-0-600-62113-3
Hardback
£12.99

Victory celebrations 1945
On August 15, 1945, after almost six years of military conflict, which covered a large part of the globe and resulted in the deaths of many millions of people, the final step with victory over Japan brought about mass celebrations throughout the country. In this cartoon, Giles captured the widespread and spontaneous outpouring of joy in the nation's capital, where tightly packed crowds milled and danced between Buckingham Palace, Whitehall, Trafalgar Square and Piccadilly Circus.

"Be funny if the siren went now wouldn't it?"

18   *Sunday Express, August 19, 1945*

Christine Keeler
The Keeler affair concerned the fact that she had been friendly at the same time with John Profumo, the British Secretary of State for War, and a Naval Attache at the Russian Embassy in London – a situation considered by the government to be a major security risk. Then, on June 20, the US Defense Secretary expressed concern that some US Air Force personnel may also have met Miss Keeler. President Kennedy arrived in London for an official visit on June 29.

"We won't detain you long, Miss Keeler. Just until all the American V.I.P.s are out of the country"

Sunday Express, June 30, 1963   87

Want more Giles? Need more Giles? If you are simply not content with just one bumper Collection then get hold of a copy of the bestselling *Giles: The Collection 2011*. A treasure-trove of wit that tickles all those familiar funny spots.

Giles: The Collection 2011
978-0-600-62119-7
Paperback
£7.99

"My wife's got a theory that it doesn't pay to let them know you're English."

Daily Express, June 24, 1953

"Repeat again, everybody: 'Mother does not want any new puppies, budgies, pussies, or bunnies for Christmas'."

Daily Express, December 16, 1977